Treasure Of Truth
God Triumphant

By
Burl L. Shepard

WORDS MATTER
P U B L I S H I N G
OUR WORDS CHANGE THE WORLD

Words Matter Publishing
P.O. Box 1190
Decatur, IL 62525
www.wordsmatterpublishing.com

ISBN 13: 978-1-958000-007

Library of Congress Catalog Card Number: 2022943862

TABLE OF CONTENTS

CHAPTER 1

"I am not ashamed of the gospel, because it is the power of God for the salvation of everyone who believes: first for the Jew, then for the Gentile. For in the gospel a righteousness from God is revealed, a righteousness that is by faith from first to last, just as it is written: The righteous will live by faith." (Romans 1:16-17 NIV)

In my previous book I wrote: "From time to time we hear accounts of people who were supposedly people of God, and who had a very large following. Through some type of revelation, these individuals were exposed to be impostors. They were interested only in the sins of the world - self, sex, power, and wealth. They will receive their just reward. Their only hope would be sincere repentance to God. Sadly, this type of transgression causes much distress and soul-searching for the people who believed in them." (*For It Is by Grace*, Page 20)

Since I wrote those words, it has been revealed that a renowned Christian apologist, by means of his power and wealth, took advantage of several women under his employment by demanding sexual favors. These women were part of an unknown business venture conducted by this man.

The term apologist does not mean that a person apologizes for the Christian faith. On the contrary, the definition of an apologist is a person who defends an idea, faith, cause, or institution. Thus, Christian apologists and atheistic apologists often debate the merits of their beliefs. The term apologetics means the branch of theology concerned with the defense or proof of Christianity. The responsibility of a Christian apologist is to answer questions in regard to the Christian faith, and then to explain the reason for their answers.

The man I am referring to spent forty years as a Christin apologist and preacher of the gospel. He was an excellent speaker and seemed to be very dedicated to the Christian faith. As a result, through his teachings and best-selling books, over the years thousands of people found Christ. The revelation in regard to this person surfaced because he had contracted a serious illness.

Only God knew the true condition of the man's soul at the time of his death on May 19, 2020. Some would say his life was a charade and he never knew

Christ. Others might say he was a true believer who made sinfully bad choices during moments of weakness, from which he could not recover. If this was the case, he is now in Heaven. God is the only determiner in such matters.

But what of the countless numbers of people that came to Christ because of him? And what of the people to which they testified who also believed? It is certain there was a snowball effect over the years of additional people who accepted Christ. Was it all in vain because of the nature of the man that gave the original message? There will be those who are not of the Christian faith that will try to make use of this for their own benefit.

A stark contrast can be made between the legacy of this man and the evangelist Billy Graham. Billy Graham has been credited with preaching the gospel to more people than anyone in history. He utilized the truth of the gospel and did not waver from its words. Billy Graham adhered to the words of the Apostle Paul written in Paul's final letter to Timothy. "All scripture is inspired by God and is useful to teach us what is true and to make us realize what is wrong in our lives. It corrects us when we are wrong and teaches us to do what is right." (2 Timothy 3:16 NLT)

Billy Graham found Christ as a young man and grew into the best known and most loved man of God of his generation. No one has equaled him, and he remained scandal-free. However, not withstanding the unblemished performance of Billy Graham and the controversy that surrounded the Christian apologist, both men achieved identical results in the preaching of God's word. That is because it is not the person speaking the word of God that achieves results, but the power of the gospel working through the speaker.

God used the words of both the Christian apologist and Billy Graham in the same way. As a result, those who found God through the Christian apologist are as secure in their salvation as those who came to God through the words of Billy Graham. No matter the circumstances, in regard to any situation, God overcomes and turns all into good for His glory.

Authors note: I did not mention the name of the Christian apologist out of general respect for the man, and of course, his family. However, the charges against him are well known throughout the Christian community. It is very sad when something of this nature happens to a man of his stature, for it causes confusion and doubt among those who believed in him. For those who are interested, there is an abundance of information available. Google RZIM-Class-Action Lawsuit, North District of Georgia.

I heard of a Christian apologist addressing a group of college students. After speaking, he conducted a question-and-answer session. One of the students asked a question in regard to Noah and the flood. The student wondered how those on the ark could have survived because of the height of the ark above sea level. If the ark came to rest on Mount Ararat as the Bible says, it would have been close to 17,000 feet above sea level. The temperature would have been very cold, and the air so thin that life could not have survived. Silence filled the room.

After thinking about this question, the Christian apologist responded that as the water continued to rise, sea level would have been calculated at the current depth of the water at any given moment. Because of this, when the ark came to rest on Mount Ararat, it would not have been almost 17,000 feet above sea level but actually at sea level. Therefore, all on the ark would not have been subjected to the extreme conditions.

That, in my opinion, was a very good answer. While I am not very fast on my feet, my first thought was God made the world and everything in it. I'm certain the Lord of Heaven and Earth would have in some supernatural way, provided for the safety and comfort of all aboard the ark. God would not have been wringing His hands, as He watched in horror those on the ark gasping for breath as they slowly froze to death.

There are those in the scientific community that have expounded the theory that the universe has conscious thought. They contend our thoughts and actions are not our own but are controlled by the universe. Are God and the universe one and the same?

God is not the universe. God created the universe and everything the universe contains. God has no beginning and has no end. The universe had a beginning and will have an end. God does not control our thoughts but gives us free will to make our own choices. The universe is not our god. He who made the universe is our God.

CHAPTER 2

How do we identify with God? God is spirit existing in what is referred to as the Trinity. The Trinity is the union of three: The Father, the Son, and the Holy Spirit existing as one but also at the same time existing as three. This has been described as the three-fold personality of the one Divine Being.

In Romans chapter three, the Bible says all have sinned and fall short of God's glory. Why is this important? "For the wages of sin is death, but the gift of God is eternal life in Christ Jesus our Lord." (Romans 6:25 NIV) Jesus Christ, or God the Son, is the way God has provided for the forgiveness of sin. The Book of John discloses much one needs to know in regard to Jesus Christ and God's love for humanity.

"In the beginning was the Word, and the Word was with God, and the Word was God. He was with God in the beginning.

Through Him all things were made; without Him nothing was made that has been made. In Him was life, and that life was the light of men. The light shines in the darkness, but the darkness has not understood it." (John 1:1-5 NIV)

It is important to understand that God did not create Jesus. Jesus is not a created being, rather he is God the Son, the second part of the Trinity. He has no beginning and has no end. Everything was created through Jesus. All life came from Him. The light that came because of Him will never be destroyed by the darkness.

"For God so loved the world that He gave His one and only Son, that whoever believes in Him shall not perish but have eternal life. For God did not send His Son into the world to condemn the world, but to save the world through Him." (John 3:16-17 NIV) God's love for humanity is so great that He gave a part of himself, God the Son, so that those who believed in His Son would not perish but live for eternity. The Son did not take human form and come into the world to judge the world but to offer redemption from sin.

"I and the Father are one." (John 10:30 NIV)

In this statement Jesus made claim to His divinity. He claimed to be God. This outraged the religious leaders and they wanted Him dead. Their laws proclaimed that anyone who claimed to be God should die. They now had the excuse they needed and started planning His death.

"I am the resurrection and the life. He who believes in Me will live, even though he dies; and whoever lives and believes in me will never die." (John 11:25-26 NIV)

This is the essence of salvation. When one believes in Christ, their spirit is assured resurrection into eternal life. At the moment of their physical death, they will immediately enter the spiritual realm. The spiritual life will not be diminished, but will be more meaningful in the presence of God.

"Do not let your hearts be troubled. Trust in God, trust also in Me. In My Father's house are many rooms; if it were not so, I would have told you. I am going there to prepare a place for you. And if I go and prepare a place for you, I will come back and take you to be with Me that you also may be where I am. You know the way to the place where I am going." (John 14: 1-4 NIV)

Jesus told His disciples not to hold onto anxious thoughts but to trust in God and Himself. He told them there was much room in Heaven for all who believe. While He would be leaving to prepare a place in Heaven for believers, He would return for them when His work was finished.

He then told His disciples they already knew the way to His Father's home. At this, Jesus was told by Thomas that actually they didn't know where He was going and had no idea how to get there. Jesus replied:

"I am the way and the truth and the life. No one comes to the Father except through Me. If you really knew Me, you would know My Father as well. From now on you do know Him and have seen Him." (John 14: 6-7 NIV)

It is very important to understand that only through Jesus the Son can one find God the Father. Jesus is both God and man, and by trusting in Him we find unity with God. "For there is one God and one mediator between God and men, the man Christ Jesus, who gave himself as a ransom for all men – the testimony given in its proper time." (1 Timothy 2: 5-6 NIV)

"If you love Me, you will obey what I command. And I will ask the Father, and He will give you another counselor to be with you forever – the Spirit of truth. The world cannot accept Him because it neither sees Him nor knows Him. But you know Him, for He lives with you and will be in you." (John 14: 15-17 NIV)

Jesus told His disciples He would soon be leaving them. Because of their faith and love for Him, they would not be left alone. God would send them the third part of the Trinity, the Holy Spirit, which is the

Spirit of God Himself. The Holy Spirit came on the disciples just before Jesus' accension into Heaven.

The Holy Spirit is present within all believers. He lives with us and in us and will never leave us. The power of the Holy Spirit activates the process of sanctification, which means to make holy and purify from sin. This will be an ongoing process throughout the lifetime of the believer as they grow and become stronger by their faith in God. At the death of the physical body, the believer's spirit will be made perfect in the presence of God.

Many people wonder about the unforgivable sin, for they fear they may have committed it. By understanding the unforgivable sin, perhaps some anxious minds will find rest. The following are sins that will be forgiven: murder, suicide, abortion, adultery, homosexuality, fornication, bestiality, prostitution, and any other sin the human mind can conceive.

What then is the unforgivable sin? As we read in John 14: 15-17, when one finds repentance with God the third part of the Trinity, the Holy Spirit, will dwell within them. However, if your physical body dies and you have not accepted Christ, by having denied the Holy Spirit access you have severed all ties with God. Salvation cannot be obtained after death. You have committed the unforgivable sin.

"And so, I tell you, every sin and blasphemy will be forgiven men, but the blasphemy against the Spirit will not be forgiven. Anyone who speaks a word against the Son of man will be forgiven, but anyone who speaks against the Holy Spirit will not be forgiven, either in this age or in the age to come." (Matthew 12: 31-32 NIV) Those who accept Christ have two birthdays, the date of their physical birth and the date they were born again in Christ Jesus.

"Each of you should look not only to your own interests, but also to the interests of others." (Philippians 2: 4 NIV) Of course we should look to our own interests. It would be foolishness, even slothfulness not to. But goodness would abound if the central theme of our interactions was "we", rather than "me".

If followed; this would have a huge impact on our various interactions. Whether in regard to religion, social issues, education or family, harmony would dominate.

CHAPTER 3

The people of Israel are people God has chosen for Himself. "I will make you into a great nation and I will bless you; I will make your name great, and you will be a blessing. I will bless those who bless you and whoever curses you I will curse; and all people on Earth will be blessed through you." (Genesis 12: 2-3 NIV)

Before the nation of Israel came into being, God chose Abram, later called Abraham, as the father of the Jewish people. When Abraham was ninety-nine years old, God told him that his wife Sarai, who was renamed Sarah, who was ninety years old and barren, would give him a son. Abraham and Sarah were to name their son Isaac. God told Abraham they would be the father and mother of nations. Abraham believed God, and it was credited to him as righteousness.

Some time after Isaac was born, God tested Abraham by telling him to sacrifice Isaac as a burnt offering. When Abraham started to carry out this command, the

Angel of the Lord, or Jesus, called out and told Abraham not to harm the boy. The Angel of the Lord, or Jesus, said to Abraham: "I swear by Myself, declares the Lord, that because you have done this and have not withheld your son, your only son, I will surely bless you and make your descendants as numerous as the stars in the sky and as the sand on the seashore. Your descendants will take possession of the cities of their enemies, and through your offspring all nations on Earth will be blessed, because you have obeyed me." (Genesis 22: 16-18 NIV) All who believe are children of Abraham.

The Jewish people were scattered through the world for many years. Biblical prophecy predicted the time would come when they would return to their homeland. Israel was formed as a Jewish state in 1948. Jerusalem is now its capital. Over the centuries, all divinely-inspired prophecy concerning Israel has come to pass: "But now I have chosen Jerusalem for My name to be there, and I have chosen David to rule my people, Israel." (2 Chronicles 6:6 NIV)

The woman said, "I know that Messiah (called Christ) is coming. When He comes, He will explain everything to us." Then Jesus declared, "I who speak to you am He." (John 4: 25-26 NIV) In general, the Jewish people have failed to accept Jesus as the Messiah, or the promised deliverer. However, Jesus is regarded by

Christians as fulfilling this promise. Jesus quoted scripture when He said, "The stone the builders rejected has become the capstone; the Lord has done this, and it is marvelous in our eyes." (Matthew 21:42 NIV) The word capstone is also referred to as cornerstone. Jesus is also referred to as "a stone that causes men to stumble and a rock that makes them fall." (Isaiah 8:14 NIV)

Because the Jewish people have not accepted Christ as the Messiah, there are many within the Christian faith that have turned to Replacement Theology. Replacement Theology is the opinion that the church is the new or true Israel and has permanently replaced Israel as the people of God. The arrogance of mortal human beings toward the Creator is unbelievable. God will never forsake His chosen people. He has absolute power, rule, and intentions. Apostasy, or the abandonment of one's religious faith is predicted in the Bible as a sign of the proximity of the end time events. The fact that so many in the religious community have turned to Replacement Theology could certainly be viewed as apostasy.

The Ten Commandments are listed for those who are not familiar with God's Law or might wish a review of His Law.

You shall have no other gods before me.

You shall not make for yourself an idol in the form of anything.

You shall not misuse the name of the Lord your God.

Remember the Sabbath Day by keeping it holy.

Honor your father and your mother.

You shall not murder.

You shall not commit adultery.

You shall not steal.

You shall not give false testimony.

You shall not covet.

(Exodus 20: 3-17 NIV)

The Law was given 430 years after Abraham received the covenant, or God's promise that all nations on Earth would be blessed through his descendants. The reason Abraham was declared righteous by the fact he believed and trusted God was because there was no Law upon which to measure his righteousness.

However, if the law had been in existence when God made the covenant, Abraham would not have been declared righteous by the Law. The reason is because of the fall of humanity, and the sinful nature that resulted from the fall, no person can live the perfect life that God demands through His law. God realized this when His Law was given to the people of Israel. Why then did God bother to give humanity His Law? If the Law cannot save us, what is its purpose?

It is important to know all who wrote scripture were inspired by the third part of the Trinity, God the Holy Spirit. God is the author of the Holy Bible. While the following passage of scripture is somewhat lengthy, it speaks volumes, and contains the information needed to understand the Law and its purpose. This passage of scripture tells us how the Law is leading to the only way of receiving redemption or deliverance from sin. It reveals that no person can be judged righteous by their own works. This passage of scripture is certainly worthy of our discernment.

"Now we know that whatever the Law says, it says to those who are under the Law, so that every mouth may be silenced and the whole world held accountable to God. Therefore, no one will be declared righteous in his sight by observing the Law; rather, through the Law we become conscious of sin.

But now a righteousness from God, apart from the Law has been made known, to which the law and the prophets testify. This righteousness from God comes through faith in Jesus Christ to all who believe. There is no difference, for all have sinned and fall short of the glory of God and are justified freely by His grace through the redemption that came by Christ Jesus. God presented him as a sacrifice of atonement through faith in His blood." (Romans 3:19-25 NIV)

The first reason the Law was given is revealed in verse 20: "Rather through the Law we become conscious of sin." Without being conscious of sin and knowing what sin is, we can only rely on self and the sinful nature of self to determine what we believe to be right or wrong. For how is a person to know it is a sin to steal, if God had not revealed this through His Law? In the same way, how is a man to know he should not covet his neighbor's wife, or a woman to know she should not covet her neighbor's husband, if God had not revealed through His Law that both to covet and to commit adultery is a sin?

The second reason for the Law is after receiving forgiveness from sin, the newly born-again believer, through the Holy Spirit, develops an understanding of the Law and develops the innate desire to follow the Law. That is why, though never perfect in this world, the born-again believer is set apart. It is by the example of their lives they are recognized as Christians.

What is the righteousness from God, apart from the Law, and how is it obtained? "He was delivered over to death for our sins and was raised to life for our justification." (Romans 4:25 NIV) Jesus Christ, God the Son who is equal to God the Father, took human form and lived the perfect sin-free life. Christ was the unblemished sacrifice for the sins of humanity.

He took our sins upon Himself, dying for them in our place so that we might live. Christ did this once for all, because once salvation has been received it can never be lost. "But God demonstrated His own love for us in this: While we were still sinners, Christ died for us." (Romans 5:8 NIV)

How is one to receive the salvation that comes from Christ Jesus? In Romans 10:4 we read: Christ is the end of the Law. In other words, Christ comes before or takes the place of the Law. Romans 3:22 states that righteousness from God comes through faith in Jesus to all who believe. What is required to receive this righteousness from God? "That if you confess with your mouth, Jesus is Lord, and believe in your heart that God raised him from the dead, you will be saved. For it is with your heart that you believe and are justified, and it is with your mouth that you confess and are saved." (Romans 10:9-10 NIV)

In your own words, confess to God that you are a lost sinner, and that you realize your need for Jesus to be Lord of your life. Acknowledge you believe Christ died for your sins and God raised Him from the dead. If you do this God will forgive you of your sins, past and future. You will then receive the third part of the Trinity, God the Holy Spirit. The Holy Spirit will be a part of you forever.

Be exceedingly grateful for what God has done for you. You have received the most precious gift ever given: "For it is by grace you have been saved, through faith, and this not from yourselves, it is the gift of God - not by works, so that no one can boast." (Ephesians 2: 8-9 NIV)

Chapter 4

There are those who speak against cremation. While there is nothing in the Bible forbidding this practice, some say it shows disrespect for the human body. The fact also is brought forward that during the Rapture of believers, the souls of believers who have died over the years, and their dead bodies which will be in some state of decay, will be united by God in a supernatural way. The occurrence of cremation would make no difference to God in bringing this to pass.

Some people have felt guilt after having the body of a loved one cremated. Also, many have gone deeply in debt because of the cost of conventional funerals. There is no reason for either guilt or financial hardship to be experienced because of controversy surrounding cremation. The loved one's place in Heaven, both body and soul, is assured by the blood of Christ and the power of God.

If a person not familiar with the Bible wished to read the Biblical account of creation, they need not worry about where to start. No online research would be necessary nor would asking guidance from someone they felt was knowledgeable in the subject. They simply need turn to the first sentence in chapter one of the Book of Genesis and begin reading. In many Bibles this is page one, but this depends on how introductory pages are numbered.

God wasted no time in giving us much to ponder. He reveals much of Himself in regard to the Trinity. The second sentence in Genesis makes reference to the third part of the Trinity, the Holy Spirit. "Now the Earth was formless and empty, darkness was over the surface of the deep, and the Spirit of God was hovering over the waters." (Genesis 1:2 NIV)

God used the plural form of Himself when speaking of the creation of humanity. "Then God said, let us make man in Our image, in Our likeness, and let them rule over the fish of the sea and the birds of the air, over the livestock, over all the Earth, and over all the creatures that move along the ground." (Genesis 1:26 NIV)

The temptation of Eve, which resulted in the fall of humanity, is recorded in the Third chapter of Genesis. In this same chapter God reveals His plan for the redemption of humanity. To Satan, God said: "And

I will put enmity between you and the woman, and between your offspring and hers; he will crush your head, and you will strike his heel." (Genesis 3:15) You will strike his heel refers to Satan's attempts to defeat Christ during his life on Earth. He will crush your head foretells Satan's defeat when Christ rose from the dead. Genesis 3:15 has been referred to as the first Gospel.

Within the first three chapters of the Book of Genesis much is revealed - the Creation, the Trinity, the fall of humanity, and God's plan for the redemption of humanity. In my bible, these are on pages one through five. The Bible contains a total of sixty-six books. My particular Bible has a total of 2,035 pages. Read the Bible of your preference, and you will find that Genesis moving forward and the Book of Revelation moving backward meet together in proclaiming the glorious Good News of Jesus Christ.

In many ways the believer should be glad when they are attacked spiritually. All being quiet on the battle front would mean they were doing little to nothing in the defense and advancement of the Gospel. Therefore, Satan would turn his attention toward those who posed a threat to him.

When the believer feels they are being bombarded by Satan and his forces, they usually are. This tells them they are in the thick of things in regard to the unseen spiritual warfare that is happening around them. During those moments they should remember that He who is in them is stronger than he who is in the world. (John 4:4)

Never forget, the Holy Spirit within us is the third part of the Trinity that created the one who is in the world. Satan must conform to the boundaries in which he has been placed. The evil one knows he was defeated by Christ on the cross, but his pride will not allow him to admit it. He will continue to fight until he meets his bitter end.

The following passage of scripture exemplifies what pride can do. It's meaning is twofold, for it shows what caused the fall of Satan as well as what led to the fall of humanity. "How you have fallen from Heaven, O morning star, son of the dawn! You have been cast down to the Earth, you who once laid low the nations! You said in your heart, 'I will ascend to Heaven; I will raise my throne above the stars of God; I will sit enthroned on the mount of assembly, on the utmost heights of the sacred mountain. I will ascend above the tops of the clouds; I will make myself like the Most High! But you are brought down to the grave, to the depths of the pit." (Isaiah 14:12-15 NIV)

Satan's rebellion against God ultimately resulted in a mighty battle. "And there was war in Heaven. Michael and his angels fought against the dragon, and the dragon and his angels fought back. But he was not strong enough, and they lost their place in Heaven. The great dragon was hurled down - that ancient serpent called the devil, or Satan, who leads the whole world astray. He was hurled to the Earth, and his angels with him." (Revelation 12:7-9 NIV)

"Therefore, rejoice, you heavens, and you who dwell in them! But woe to the Earth and the sea because the devil has gone down to you! He is filled with fury, because he knows that his time is short." (Revelation 12:12 NIV)

The events recorded in Genesis chapter three in regard to the fall of humanity are real. However, there are those who believe the reference to Satan being a serpent is a symbolic term. In Revelation chapter twelve, Satan is referred to symbolically as both a dragon and a serpent.

Satan's rank was above all other angels God created. While their numbers are not revealed, many believe there are billions of these Heavenly beings. In Isaiah chapter twelve, Satan is referred to as the morning star and son of the dawn. His beauty, along with the power God granted him, was Satan's downfall. His prideful nature and love of self caused him to believe he could be like God. Because of this, his fall was swift and with him he took one-third of the angels that had chosen to follow him. It was much more than a serpent Adam and Eve encountered in the Garden.

But, what about these two? Are we to picture a naked man and woman wandering about tending a beautiful garden? I believe they were clothed in the Glory of God and possessed abilities we can not imagine. The encounter between Satan, Adam, and Eve was between three magnificent beings created by God. Satan had already fallen and was destined for Hell. By crafty deceit he caused the man and his wife to come to grief. Thus, they were no longer clothed in the Glory of God, but lay bare before Him. Paradise was indeed lost.

There are those who say they would be wary of a person who claimed to have heard the audible voice of God. I would be too. I'm not saying it's impossible, for God can do all things. If He wanted to talk to someone in an audible fashion, He would, and would not ask for permission from skeptics before doing so.

I feel certain that Jesus has appeared in dreams of countless people in order to convey information or revelations. I believe this is happening worldwide, especially in regard to those who are experiencing religious persecution. There are many in countries where the Gospel cannot be preached openly who are turning to Christ because of personal communication from Him through dreams.

I've heard people say they would also be cautious of someone following their heart. What believers must follow is the silent voice of the Holy Spirit, but the Holy Spirit and the heart work together in unison. The heart shines forth the character and essence of an individual. I believe the heart contains the soul and spirit of a human, and for that reason I feel comfortable in saying that I follow my heart. "Love the Lord your God with all your heart and with all your soul and with all your mind." (Matthew 22:37 NIV) "Who may ascend the hill of the Lord? Who many stand in His holy place? He who has clean hands and a pure heart, who does not lift up his soul to an idol or swear by what is false." (Psalm 24:3-4 NIV)

A double message is given in regard to the following passage of scriptures. The first several words imply a theme of Christmas and the gift of salvation that was given to humanity. The passage then quickly moves forward to the eternal rule of Jesus after the Second Coming. "For to us a child is born, to us a son is given, and the government will be on his shoulders. And he will be called Wonderful Counselor, Mighty God, Everlasting Father, Prince of Peace. Of the increase of his government and peace there will be no end." (Isaiah 9:6-7 NIV)

CHAPTER 5

"Come now, let us reason together" says the Lord. "Though your sins are like scarlet, they shall be as white as snow; though they are red as crimson, they shall be like wool." (Isaiah 1:18 NIV)

That God would seek out humanity is incredible. As He would have done for the Israelites many years ago, He will do today for all who believe. The depth of depravity will be forgiven those who turn to Christ.

"No eye has seen, no ear has heard, no mind has conceived what God has prepared for those who love Him." (1 Corinthians 2:9 NIV)

What will the believer experience after death, and what will Heaven be like? While one can only speculate, perhaps we should follow our hearts and see where this might lead.

The believer found himself walking along a path. He remembered nothing that had transpired leading to this moment. He did, however, realize he was no longer in the physical world. He felt as though a heavy weight had been removed and experienced a natural and welcomed lightness. His feet seemed to be barley touching the path as he moved along, yet he was in complete control of his movements. He realized an affliction, the cause of severe pain for many years, now seemed to no longer exist.

As he continued on, his vision become somewhat distorted. What seemed to be an array of pulsating waves appeared before and around him. However, he felt no fear and continued along the path. The believer first thought he was surrounded by angels and the pulsating waves were for camouflage so the Heavenly beings would not be seen. But as he continued on he understood this was not the case. The believer now realized he was walking toward Jesus, and the pulsating waves were energy that came forth from the Son of God.

Without hesitation the believer continued along the path. Having accepted Christ as his Savior many years before he felt no doubt or dismay, but the foresight of growing expectancy. Suddenly he stopped. "Oh!" How else could he possibly express his emotions for what was before him? "The Son is the radiance of God's glory and the exact representation of His being, sustaining all things by His powerful word." (Hebrews 1:3 NIV)

The Believer worshipped the Lord and interacted with Him in a glorious way. The glow from the warmth and compassion Jesus had shown lingered still. He had received a cherished impression of unconditional love and with it the wonderful knowledge he would never again be separated from God.

The believer now stood before a large span of water with a vastness he felt was measureless. The water's surface was as smooth as glass, and as his gaze fell across it, he was struck by its whiteness. The water appeared to be as white as snow.

The shoreline upon which the believer stood was dotted by large boulders. On occasion the smoothness of the water in the area of a boulder was interrupted by a swirling that caused the water to go airborne before crashing down on the boulder. The believer was puzzled for he saw no cause for this.

This happened to a boulder near the believer. A soft, gentle breeze carried mist from the splashing water, and it fell upon the believer. He experienced a pleasant tingling sensation from the mist. Thus, drawn to the boulder the believer approached and stood next to it. As he stood watching, the water swirled before going airborne high above the believer. Again, he felt no fear. In fact, the believer wanted this water for he sensed it was needed before he would be able to continue his journey. He stood firmly as he watched the water go high before cascading down as if he was standing beneath a waterfall.

The effect was immediate. While his sins had been forgiven because of Jesus on the cross, the guilt and shame of those sins had remained. Satan caused the memories to surface when least expected, causing doubt to creep in and his faith to waiver. While his recent interaction with Jesus had certainly erased all doubts, the cleansing power of the water had erased all memories of his sins. The believer understood. Not even the memory of evil would be present in Heaven. He knew that he had been changed by God. While he was the same in essence, he was also different. He now had not only the forgiveness for sin but was free from the bondage of the memory of sin.

Unexpectedly, the believer found himself over the water. While he knew not how, he knew that he was moving effortlessly toward what he knew was The Other Side. Suddenly, he saw the angels. They were magnificent beings, going to and fro between Heaven and Earth as they caried out missions assigned by God. While invisible to people on Earth unless God specified otherwise, the believer now realized they were visible to all in the spiritual realm. The believer's presence was not acknowledged by the angels, but he thought that might change when Heaven's shore was reached.

The vastness of the water soon yielded to a stunningly beautiful landscape. The believer saw a variety of trees, bushes, and flowers growing in profusion of lavish, uniform order. The sky was cloudless. There was no sun, but brightness prevailed. The believer knew no sun was needed, for the brightness was caused by the glory of God. Animals moved about and children played. Adults watched and at times interacted with the children. Clothing was colorful and loose-fitting.

The believer saw several people that were standing in a group, watching, and pointing in his direction. His course instantly changed, taking him directly toward the watching and apparently excited group of people. As the believer grew near his spiritual heart leapt with jubilant excitement for there were many within the group he recognized. He instinctively realized the relatives and ancestors within the group he did not know were those who had arrived in Heaven either during his early childhood, or before his physical birth. Soon, tears of joy, the only kind Heaven allows, were shed, as all in the group rejoiced and praised their Heavenly Father because of the arrival of their loved one.

The believer's spirit has arrived in Heaven and has been reunited with his loved ones. Now, what might he expect from his spiritual existence? While the worship of God will be foremost, imagine what good things you would do for someone you loved if you had the ability. How much more our Heavenly Father will do for us, and HE HAS THE ABILITY. There will be spiritual growth and maturity, as well as random interaction with Heaven's inhabitants. But there will be much more. It will be a very meaningful existence.

In regard to where we might reside, one can only surmise. Perhaps it will be as follows: "He who dwells in the shelter of the Most High, will rest in the shadow of the Almighty." (Psalm 91:1) I am certain it will not be large mansions and swimming pools. We will have no need of that.

The sound of laughter will be frequent, and the aroma and taste of coffee will be, well heavenly. Our senses will be intensified and enhanced so that food and drink, though not needed for our survival, will be enjoyed to the fullest. We will have the opportunity to pursue whatever worthwhile endeavors we might choose without the burden of time or schedule. Our spiritual minds will be clear and at peace as we dwell in the presence of God.

There will be no end to what we might expect. I heard a preacher once say: "There will be animals in Heaven, but they will not be the pets we had on Earth." Says who? Many beloved pets, at this very moment, might be patiently awaiting their owner's arrival. "Who knows if the spirit of man rises upward and if the spirit of the animals goes down into the Earth?" (Ecclesiastes 3:21 NIV) God can and will bring good things to pass for those who love Him.

There are those who wonder about the statement of Jesus when He made reference to marriage in Heaven. They cannot understand why they would not be allowed to still be married to an Earthly spouse they love very much. "When the dead rise, they will neither marry nor be given in marriage; they will be like the angels in Heaven." (Mark 12:25 NIV)

The spirits and souls of believers who have died are now in Heaven. During the Rapture, they will receive glorified bodies that are much different than our Earthly bodies. Marriage as we now know it will no longer exist. However, perhaps former spouses who choose, will experience a spiritual union that results in a much deeper bonding and meaning than what was experienced on Earth. This spiritual union would continue throughout eternity.

CHAPTER 6

The Heaven we have been contemplating will not be the final home for believers. Earth will be the final home, but it will be a different Earth from the one that now exists. Buckle your seat belt before we continue, and we will briefly probe what is referred to as the End Time Events.

Eschatology is the study of Bible prophecy. I believe in order for prophecy to be fulfilled, the events described in the Bible are literal occurrences. There are differences of opinion in regard to this. Believers should study God's Word, allow themselves to be led by the Holy Spirit, and follow their hearts. The main thing is to not lose sight of Christ and the deliverance from sin He offers.

The Rapture will be the beginning of the End Time Events. One meaning of the word "rapture" is to be transported to another place or sphere of existence. God will, in an instant, transfer what is referred to as The Bride of Christ, also known as the Church, to Heaven. The term "Church" is not referring to any particular church of denominations, but rather to all true born-again believers. There will be many in all churches and denominations that will not be taken during the Rapture, because they are not true born-again Christians. This event will be unexpected and will happen very quickly. It will not be seen by those left behind. There will be much chaotic disorder, as people search for an explanation for the sudden disappearance of great numbers of people on a worldwide scale.

During the Rapture, all living Christians will be taken up and transported alive to Heaven and will then be with Christ forever. The dead bodies of all believers who had died over the years will be resurrected and united with their souls and spirits which had been residing in Heaven. It will not matter about decay of the bodies, or even if some bodies have been completely destroyed. God will bring this unity about in a supernatural way. The believers body will be similar to the glorified body of Christ.

Infants, children, the mentally challenged, and those who have not reached the age of accountability will be included in the Rapture. While there is no biblical reference in regard to this, common sense tells us God will not forsake the innocent. "People were also bringing babies to Jesus to have Him touch them.

When the disciples saw this, they rebuked them. But Jesus called the children to him and said, 'Let the little children come to me, and do not hinder them, for the kingdom of God belongs to such as these.'" (Luke 18:15-16 NIV) In regard to the innocent other than infants and children: "The Lord will fulfill his purpose for me. Your love O Lord endures forever. Do not abandon the works of your hands." (Psalm 138: NIV)

The purpose of the Rapture will be for Christ to remove His bride, or all true believers, from the Earth before the seven-year Tribulation Period begins. Those who are not followers of Christ, and are left behind, will face much deceit during the first half of the Tribulation. The second half will be a period of unparalleled suffering upon the Earth the likes of which has never before been experienced.

After the Rapture has occurred, and independently of anything that is happening on Earth, the Judgment Seat of God will take place. This will be in regard to those who were already in Heaven and whose bodies were resurrected during the Rapture, as well as those taken alive. It will have nothing to do with any losing their salvation, for salvation once received can never be taken.

The Judgment Seat of God will be conducted by Jesus. Awards will be given in accordance with each believer's service to God. Some will receive much, and some will receive little. Some will be asked why they did not do more, or why they were completely inactive in regard to their service to Him. During this time, there will be personal interaction with Jesus.

The Second Coming of Jesus will end the seven-year Tribulation Period. All those with resurrected bodies, as well as the living raptured will accompany Christ to Earth. This is where they will reside during the 1,000-year reign of Christ on Earth.

During the Second Coming, the devil will be bound and thrown into the abyss for 1,000 years. Jesus will rule on Earth with perfect justice and righteousness during this period of time. After the 1,000 years have passed, the devil will be released for a short period of time. Even after the perfect rule of Jesus, the devil will entice some to attack God's chosen people, Israel. God will destroy those attacking Israel with fire from the sky.

One might wonder why, after 1,000 years of perfect peace, righteousness and justice brought about by the rule of Jesus, there would still be those who would follow Satan. All those who are Raptured will be given glorified bodies that are similar to the body of Christ. These bodies will never die, and they will not have the ability to procreate. However, during the Tribulation, there will be some that were left behind who will ask for God's forgiveness and become followers of Christ.

These born-again believers will enter the 1,000-year reign of Christ in natural bodies. These people will have the ability to procreate and will repopulate the Earth, for millions will perish during the Tribulation.

While these believers' salvation is assured, their descendants will be born with the sinful nature. Some of these will turn to God and be saved. Others will rebel, wanting to be their own god and live by their own rules. These are the ones who will follow Satan during the attack on Israel. If anything bears witness to the destructive power of sin it is this.

After this, the Great White Throne Judgment will occur. Satan will meet his doom as he and his fallen angels are thrown into the lake of burning sulfur. The souls of those who did not believe, and reside in the abode of the dead, will be awakened to face judgment. "Then Earth and the grave were thrown into the lake of fire. This lake of fire is the second death." Revelation 20:14 NLT)

"Don't be afraid of those who want to kill your body; they cannot touch your soul. Fear only God, who can destroy both soul and body in Hell." (Matthew 10:28 NLT) "The second death is spiritual death, meaning either eternal torment or destruction. In either case it is permanent separation from God." Commentary: Tyndale, Life Application Study Bible, New Living Translation, Large Print, Page 2882.

After God's judgment, the current Heaven and Earth are no more, and the new Heaven and new Earth come into existence. "Then I saw a new Heaven and a new Earth, for the first Heaven and the first Earth had passed away, and there was no longer any sea. I saw the Holy City, the new Jerusalem coming down out of Heaven from God, prepared as a bride beautifully dressed for her husband. And I heard a loud voice from the throne saying, 'Now the dwelling of God is with men, and he will live with them. They will be his people, and God Himself will be with them and be their God. He will wipe every tear from their eyes. There will be no more death or mourning or crying or pain, for the old order of things has passed away." (Revelation 21:1-4 NIV) This marvelous thing God has done will change everything, for as the saying goes, it's a whole new ball game.

CHAPTER 7

The 1,000-year reign of Jesus on Earth has ended. This was a finite, measurable amount of time. We now have the infinite, endlessness of eternity before us. God has eliminated all evil. All that remain are born-again children of God, and all have glorified bodies. Before us lie the new Heaven and the new Earth. The prospects that are before us are as endless as the time we will have to pursue them. What can humanity expect now that humanity has been reunited with God and once more has access to the Tree of Life?

We will continue to grow spiritually, and our worship of God will be paramount. While we will never come close to equaling God's holiness, we will continuously expand our capacity to love, for love will be the direction in which all things progress.

Idleness is not the nature of God, nor will idleness be the ways of His people. We will be free to pursue worthwhile endeavors in which we are interested. We will not be restricted in numbers of endeavors nor time, for we will have endless flow of forever before us.

But, while the new Earth will be our home, we will not be confined to it. There is a new universe before us. Who can begin to imagine the wonderful mysteries God has created? For those who desire, there will be no limit of their ability to reach far away galaxies. But how will we accomplish this?

To help understand the vastness of the universe, consider the fact that the speed of light is 186,000 miles per second. If it were 186,000 miles per hour, it would be incredible, but I am talking seconds. The distance light travels in a year based on the speed of 186,000 miles per second, is referred to as one light year. While it is difficult to comprehend, there are galaxies in the universe that would take millions of light years to reach. One would need to take more than a sack lunch for such a journey.

But maybe there's a better way. Imagine a white strip of cloth that is twelve inches long and one inch wide. At each end of the imaginary strip of cloth, in the center, there is a black dot. One black dot represents the new Earth, and the other black dot represents a planet in a faraway galaxy. The distance between the two dots represents the time and space between the two planets.

Using your mind's eye, take the imaginary white strip of cloth and fold it from its center so that the two ends are even, and the two black dots are touching. Now, how far apart are the two planets? By bending space and time, a journey that would have taken millions of light years has suddenly become a step away. It seems we would not need to pack a lunch after all.

This is one example of how God might dispatch those who wish to explore the universe. But I am using the measurements of man. The measurements of God, the One who created all things seen and unseen, would be vastly different. For example, His inclination might be to simply send the explorers at some unimaginable super speed to the intended destination. Or it might be God will give us the ability to travel by thought alone.

We may not give enough credit to what our God can do. The One who created all things has complete control over His creation. How can we know the richness of life that was available to Adam and his wife before the fall? Now, once again humanity will be free from sin, and the fact that free will and a sinful nature make a dreadful combination. God will again bring together what has been lost.

Chapter 8

It is recorded in the Book of Luke that shortly before His arrest, while praying on the Mount of Olives, Jesus sweated drops of blood. This is a rare clinical condition and is brought about by severe anguish and anxiety. "And being in anguish, he prayed more earnestly, and his sweat was like drops of blood falling to the ground." (Luke 22:44 NIV)

If Jesus the human man was ever going to say: "Enough, they're not worth it!" it would have been at that moment. But, knowing full well the horror He was about to experience by His crucifixion, Jesus stood firm and continued on to die for the sins of humanity, therefore fulfilling the purpose of the Incarnation.

We do not fully understand the love that was shown, for we could not bear the guilt of fully understanding our sinful nature. The perfect man gave perfect obedience to God and fulfilled the purpose for which He had been born. "Then I said, 'Here I am - it is written about me in the scroll - I have come to do your will, O God.'" (Hebrews 10:7 NIV)

In 2 Timothy, the Apostle Paul describes the personal nature of many non-believers during the period of time leading to the last days. As we read His description in regard to the traits of these people, we can see a mirror-image of what is occurring in various locations throughout America and the world.

"But mark this: There will be terrible times in the last days. People will be lovers of themselves, lovers of money, boastful, proud, abusive, disobedient to their parents, ungrateful, unholy, without love, unforgiving, slanderous, without self-control, brutal, not lovers of the good, treacherous, rash, conceited, lovers of pleasure rather than lovers of God - having a form of godliness but denying its power. Have nothing to do with them." (2 Timothy 3:1-5 NIV)

In regard to America, not only are we a divided country, we have allowed foreign enemies to mingle among us. We have formed dependency on them while allowing them to purchase large tracts of our country. The sad truth is America has been invaded from within.

Those elected and appointed to represent the American people must do so. They must not yield to fear or pursue their own special interests. The fact that a federal judge can put forth a ruling that is based on their personal opinion and that affects the entire country speaks volumes.

The following quote from Abraham Lincoln has many times been used out of context. These words, when written, were in regard to issues unrelated to those we face today. However, the words ring true, and are an accurate description of today's America. "America will never be destroyed from the outside. If we falter and lose our freedom, it will be because we destroyed ourselves."

"A new command I give you: Love one another. As I have loved you, so you must love one another. By this all men will know that you are my disciples if you love one another." (John 13:34-35 NIV) Inhumanity toward fellow humans has prevailed periodically over the course of history. Many times the gospel has been restrained through the power of sin. However, the power of the gospel has persevered, marching ever forward according to God's purpose. The central theme of love was brought forth by the man Christ Jesus.

There are those in today's culture who believe it is possible to find God other than through Jesus. The belief we could in some way accomplish this without the blood of Christ is wrong in regard to secular reasoning and is apostasy in regard to supposed believers. Only the power of the gospel and what Jesus accomplished on the cross will lead to God and eternal life.

What is the purpose of our lives? "From one man He made every nation of men, that they should inhabit the whole Earth; and He determined the times set for them and the exact places where they should live. God did this so that men would seek Him and perhaps reach out for Him and find Him, though He is not far from each one of us." (Acts 17:26-27 NIV)

He is not far from each one of us, a loving God, a loving Father, calling His children home. Redemption is assured by the death of Jesus on the cross. By the act of His sacrifice, Jesus took our sins upon Himself. No matter what you have done, if you ask, you will be forgiven. Are you concerned about the surreal conditions across America and throughout the world? The swiftness associated with current conditions was frightening. There are powerful forces at work, unyielding in their determination for power and control.

As if current world conditions are not enough, do you have feelings of guilt about things you have done? This is a common human condition instilled by God and its purpose is to draw people to Him. This can be equated to our conscience. If you have come to the point of believing you need God, but have issues that are holding you back, consider what the Bible does not say in regard to salvation. The Word of God does not say believe this, this, this, and this and you will be saved. On the contrary, it does not matter if you believe the world is six thousand years old or six billion years old. Nor does it matter what you believe about the Rapture or the Second Coming of Jesus. There are disagreements about these things, and more.

The fact is God's Word says one thing and one thing only is required for salvation. Nothing else will do. What is the one thing? As I have already alluded to, this is explained in the Book of Romans. Because of its significance, this important passage of Scripture deserves to be repeated. "That if you confess with your mouth, Jesus is Lord, and believe in your heart that God raised Him from dead, you will be saved. For it is with your heart that you believe and are justified, and it is with your mouth that you confess and are saved." (Romans 10:910 NIV) If you are sincere and ask for forgiveness, by the blood of Christ, forgiveness will be given.

Herein lies the most important decision a person can make. Our physical lives are no more than the blink of an eye when compared to eternity. For the believer what lies ahead is existence as God intended. However, life is uncertain and can end in an instant. Do not commit the only sin that will not be forgiven.

Remember, salvation cannot be obtained after death. One must ask for forgiveness, and allow the Holy Spirit access, while in the physical realm.

My prayer is that you will make the correct decision, for your future will then be secure. Nothing in Heaven or on Earth can ever take God's love and what Jesus did on the cross from those who are born again. There will always be a mystery in regard to God. All truth God intends for those who believe will be revealed, if not in this life, in the life to come. For once Christ is found, all else will fall into place.

May God Bless
Burl L. Shepard